IMAGES
of America

WALWORTH
COUNTY FAIR

Taylor Pipes

Copyright ©2005 by Taylor Pipes
ISBN 0-7385-3445-5

Published by Arcadia Publishing
Charleston SC, Chicago IL, Portsmouth NH, San Francisco CA

Printed in Great Britain

Library of Congress Catalog Card Number: 20059424876

For all general information contact Arcadia Publishing at:
Telephone 843-853-2070
Fax 843-853-0044
E-mail sales@arcadiapublishing.com
For customer service and orders:
Toll-Free 1-888-313-2665

Visit us on the internet at http://www.arcadiapublishing.com

To my father, who has instilled in me an unwavering love of history.

Contents

Acknowledgments		6
Introduction		7
1.	Birth of a Fair	9
2.	Souvenirs of Fairs Past	23
3.	Planes, Trains, and Automobiles	37
4.	Postcards from the Walworth County Fair	49
5.	Judgement Day	67
6.	Time for a Parade	75
7.	Harnessing a Tradition	87
8.	Live in Concert	99
9.	Changing Times	103
10.	Life of a Carnie	109
11.	The Modern Fair	115

ACKNOWLEDGMENTS

There are many people to thank; if it were not for them, this book would not have become a reality. A very special thank you to the Walworth County Fair, the board, and especially Susan Pruessing for allowing me complete access to the vast collections of photographs, books, and other fair paraphernalia. Without those sources, the book would be severely lacking in its scope, and this project stemmed from my hope to share the extensive history of one of the country's best fairs.

This book would not have been possible without the support of the Walworth County Fair Foundation—board members and more than 6,000 members ensure that the fair will be around for the next century. The board was founded on November 1, 2001, and has established an endowment fund for future fair needs, as well as developing programs that keep fairgoers coming back. This foundation truly recognizes the widespread acclaim the fair has received, and works hard so that both the event and the property attached to it become more successful and fruitful with each passing year.

Many thanks to Doris Reinke for her vast knowledge of Elkhorn history and for allowing access to even more relics of Walworth County Fair's past. The photographs and postcards she provided (belonging to the Walworth County Historical Society) are numerous in the publication.

A special thank you for the photographs provided by Frank Eames, which have appeared in past issues of the *Elkhorn Independent*. My curious nature led me into your print shop in Elkhorn, and from this meeting, I was able to secure some incredible views of the fair seen from the eyes of *Independent* reporters.

Thanks to Mary and Tom Amon of Elkhorn for providing me family photographs of the antique car parade.

A huge thank you to my editor, Elizabeth Beachy; if it were not for my chance phonecall about my idea, this project would never have been given the green light. Your support and guidance throughout this process were amazing no matter what continent I was working from!

Also, thanks to Jon Amon, Paul Gebauer, and Travis Pipes; our endless wandering each year at the fair fully established my love of the event from an early age and made this project both an endeavor to preserve history and a fond visit back to our recent youth.

Finally, thanks to my family for their support. Dad, if it were not for your computer mastery, I would have not had a scanner to make this book possible. Thanks for your watchful eye and input and your genuine interest in my lifelong dream to become published. Thanks to Jason Pipes forlending a second scanner and for input. And thank you to my Mom, for driving me to the airport from my weekend trip home to research the project.

INTRODUCTION

Elkhorn has a treasure in the Walworth County Fair. Every Labor Day weekend, the fair draws hundreds of thousands of visitors for the six-day event. It is the single biggest event in Elkhorn and Walworth County, and fairgoers travel from far away to visit and partake in the traditions that were set in motion back on a patch of land southwest of the courthouse square in 1851. The seeds of interest in those both far and near are set from childhood, as families have passed down the tradition of fairgoing for generations.

The foundation of the fair started as an exhibition and opportunity for locals to show off vegetables, fruits, and livestock, based on a constitution adopted by the Walworth County Agricultural Society in 1842. In 1855, land for the current fairgrounds was purchased on 6 acres at a hefty price of $100 per acre. Since those beginnings, the fairgrounds have expanded to almost 100 acres; the city has embraced them and grown from the east around them.

One of the earliest forms of entertainment and a critical success to the picturesque history of the Walworth County Fair was horse racing. Long ago, horses were a crucial component of both farming and transportation. As methods to improve hauling and travel increased, so too did the ability to use horses for recreation, and harness racing became wildly popular. Farmers and people from all over the Midwest recognized the high-paying purses that were handed out to winners of various heats, and their journeys to the fairgrounds quickly put Elkhorn on the racing map. In many circles, the fair was long considered to have the largest amphitheater grandstand on one of the longest and fastest half-mile ovals in the world. Today, the track is composed of limestone and still draws harness-racing fans, along with spectators for a demolition derby, truck and tractor pulls, and a series of fair concerts that turn the track into a focal point of the fair each Labor Day.

The original grandstand was not covered with a roof until almost 1896. Seventy-five years later, in the summer of 1970, the fairgrounds and their important place in the hearts of Elkhorn and Walworth County were tested. A fire destroyed the stands completely, and with only months to spare until the next fair, the community came together to establish temporary seating and set in motion a donation fund to build again. The current grandstand, composed of steel and concrete, is a symbol of the continued place in history which grandstand events at the fair have held.

Not without its share of tragedy, the fair also faced three fires, the two most serious destroyed not only the grandstand, but also a horse stable, killing more than twenty race horses and a groom.

The city's history of band instrument production also connected with the fair; the Elkhorn city band performed alongside the company of cornet and city bands from all across southern Wisconsin. They paraded in front of packed audiences during the annual parade to kickoff the fair.

Trains also had a part in building the recognition and popularity of the fair, starting in the early 1900s. Elkhorn's roots as a major transportation crossroads first began to grow when numerous trains made regular stops in the city. People could regularly travel to Milwaukee and Chicago by transfer, and even take the Southwest Limited to Kansas City with sleeping accommodations. Since Elkhorn was already a stop on many services, it was only natural when trains began shuttling fairgoers from far away, especially Chicago, where a special "lake train" took passengers right to the fair. That service ended in 1926, but only due to the high amount of fairgoers who decided to drive to the fair. Images of cars packed into the track infield and surrounding lots have not changed since. Eventually all train service ended; the last was offered on the Eagle spur, a track that entered the southeast side of the fairgrounds.

Careful planning and consideration have long made the fair in Elkhorn a favorite and highly-anticipated tradition. In fact, it is one of the few fairs that bans alcohol; the original lease contract of the fairgrounds property stated that any sales of alcohol would nullify the lease—ever since, the reputation of being a family fair has held.

Today, the planners face continued challenges in keeping attendance growing each year; the key to upholding the massive attendance for a county fair lies in its connection to children from an early age. In any event, the fair has already built on its success by making changes no other fairs have attempted, including numerous contests and activities that continue to set the fair apart from all others, ensuring that the Walworth County Fair will have a place in the memories of young and old for the next century.

One
Birth of a Fair

A woman shields her eyes from the sun with an umbrella as she heads to the grandstand in the late 1800s. To her left, a sign at the concession stand advertises the sale of ginger ale and cream soda.

This ribbon from the Walworth County Agricultural Society dates back to 1851; it has managed to survive the years despite signs of tearing.

Just as at a baseball game or a circus, this man sells balloons to patrons at the fair. As he paces the fairgrounds, he smokes a cigar.

Three unidentified men eat large slices of watermelon in the September sun. Today, fairgoers are treated not only to fruit, but to foods that are battered, fried, baked, and frozen.

The fair is over, and the difficult task of cleaning up is under way in this image from the late 1800s. Today, large trucks, street sweepers, and powerful hoses make the fair easier to clean than in this photograph, when horses and flatbed carriages were employed to haul out trash and take down tents.

A bearded man sells his wares on the midway.

A man stands next to an unidentified woman in a doorway. This entry could lead up to the grandstand in this 1916 photograph.

A poem by an unknown author in 1881 titled "The Walworth County Fair" shows one person's affinity and affection for the annual event.

> **Walworth County Fair.**
> Here at the Agricultural show,
> Are fruits and flowers of every hue,
> And delicate shades that stain the bow
> Woven of rain when the sun is aglow.
> Fragrant petals, red, white and blue.
> The roses flame, and the lilies snow,
> Peaches, soft orbs of rosea and gold:
> Quinces, touched with a mellow light:
> Apples, the boughs were proud to hold:
> Pears, shaped like bells the prairies tolled
> Plums, that might tempt an anchorite:
> Grapes, clear as raindrops, in clusters ro..
> Samples of sifted rye and wheat:
> Golden Ears of Indian Corn:
> Home-made bread that a King might eat,
> Rolls of butter, delicious and sweet,
> Honey as clear as a cloudless morn,
> At every turn at the Fair we meet.

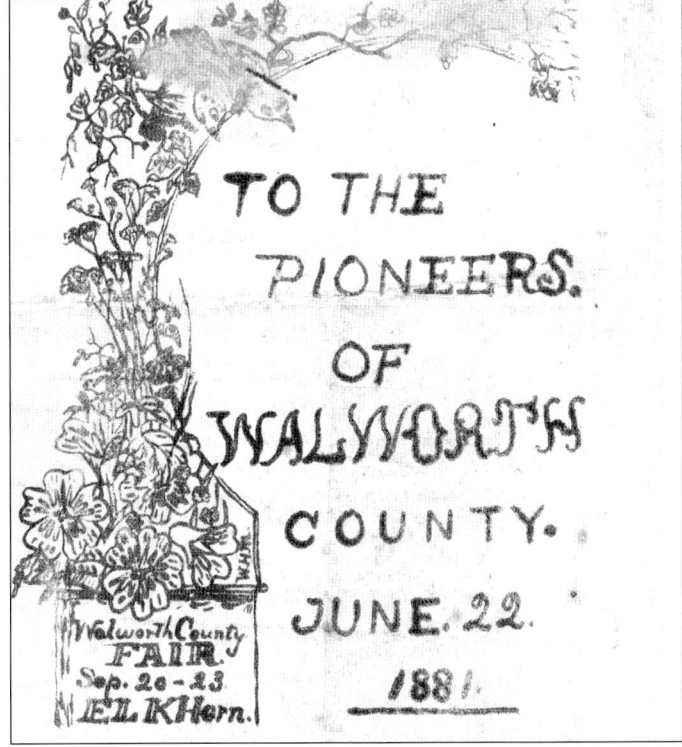

The cover of this poem shows one of the earliest advertisements for the 1881 edition of the fair on September 20–23.

A man pokes his head into the frame while a horse-drawn carriage drives along the track in this late 1800s image.

Workers attend to construction with updates being made to the grandstand. This photograph captures improvements that were made to the amphitheater, which included the addition of a rooftop canopy.

Another full crowd jams into the original grandstand. Notice the windows at the very top that offered those in the nosebleed seats a chance to take the occasional glance onto the midway, located below. The style of dress is drastically different from attire seen at today's fairs: men wear suit coats and ties, while women wear dresses and ornate hats. Two men in the front row happen to be looking directly at the camera; their haunting gazes are captured forever.

Those not fortunate enough to get under the canopy of the grandstand shield the bright sun from their eyes with black umbrellas. Since there are people standing on the track, this may have been a baseball game or some type of ceremony rather than the usual horse races. This photograph was captured from the south portion of the track, looking north.

Ribbons have been worn by officials at the fair throughout the years. This one dates back to 1896 and could have been donned by a representative of the fair or the fair board.

Another view looking southwest shows the midway and what is known as "Dining Hall Row," the permanent buildings that feed the fairgoers. Before the advent of mobile food trailers and concession stands, these buildings, often staffed and run by Walworth County churches or other organizations, served the masses. Some of these buildings are still standing today. The Elkhorn Congregational Society building in the center of Dining Hall Row currently shows antique exhibits during the fair. Take note of the band playing on a stage. Events at the grandstand cost a mere twenty-five cents; however they were more expensive than today's cost—free!

This turn-of-the-century fair advertisement proclaims "The Best County Fair," in 1903.

W. P. DUNLAP, President.
T. H GRBER, Vice-President.
SAMUEL MITCHELL, Secretary
P. L. PURDY, Sup't of Grounds.

The Best County Fair

AT

ELKHORN, WIS.

SEPTEMBER 15, 16, 17, 18,

1903.

"Don't Forget the Dates"

Before large crowds gathered for rock and country performers, audiences were wowed by horse racing and stock parades. This photograph taken from across the track shows an angle of the original grandstand not commonly seen. As the handwriting on the image indicates, the picture was taken during the fair of 1916.

A group of women joke and laugh as they hold a banner advertising the Walworth County Fair. This banner shows that the 1917 fair was held over four days.

A man walks alone at the fairgrounds. The allure of different booths and the smells drifting from all parts of the grounds are most likely the same now as they were back then; the smell of sheep and other animals might have been strong in this area, as the sheep barn is located in the background to the right.

This photograph shows relics of fairgrounds past. The closest building was the Art Hall, which was razed in the 1960s, and the building directly behind it was the famed Floral Hall, which was destroyed by a fire of unknown origin on November 2, 1933.

This virtual tent city on the main midway of the Walworth County Fair in the early 1900s looks strikingly similar to the layout of recent fairs. The Treasury Building can be seen in the background, and fairgoers stroll the midway and sit on a bench while eating at a food booth

An aerial image of the fair shows that the layout of the grounds and the oval track haven't changed much. The main differences are that Highway 43 does not exist and the boundary of town has not reached quite so far. The main highway leading into town is Highway 11.

Not only was George Wylie sheriff for many years, he also served on the fair board at the Walworth County Fair. Here he sits sternly on his horse; he was a fixture all over the fairgrounds, especially near the racetrack.

Fair personnel stand with a watchful eye over the day's festivities to make sure everything is going as planned.

A funeral program shows the devotion Wilson E. MaGill had for the fair as he stands in front of the Fair Dining Hall and the Educational Building on the grounds. MaGill is now buried in Hazel Ridge Cemetery on the western edge of Elkhorn.

The center of the infield is packed to the track with cars and spectators. Notice the tower rising prominently off the center of the home stretch of the track; it was used to judge events and later to call the action of horse racing and to announce parades to the audience.

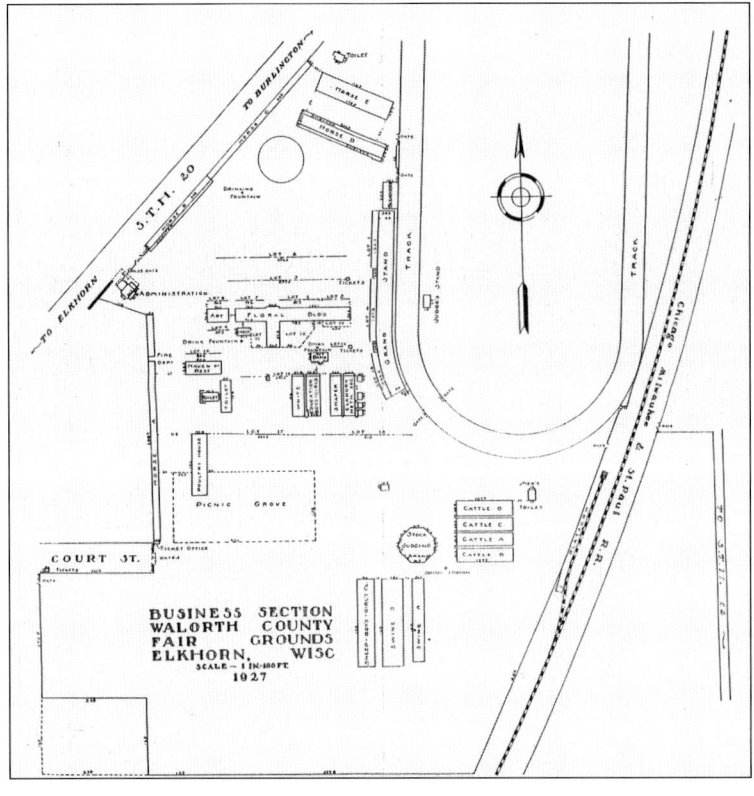

An eagle's eye view of the fairgrounds on paper shows all the buildings that sprinkled the landscape in 1927. The dotted line on the right of the map shows the Eagle Branch of the Chicago, Milwaukee & St. Paul Railroad and the platform where passengers were dropped off and picked up daily. Besides the grandstand, the largest building on the grounds was the Floral Hall building located in the center of the map.

Two
Souvenirs of Fairs Past

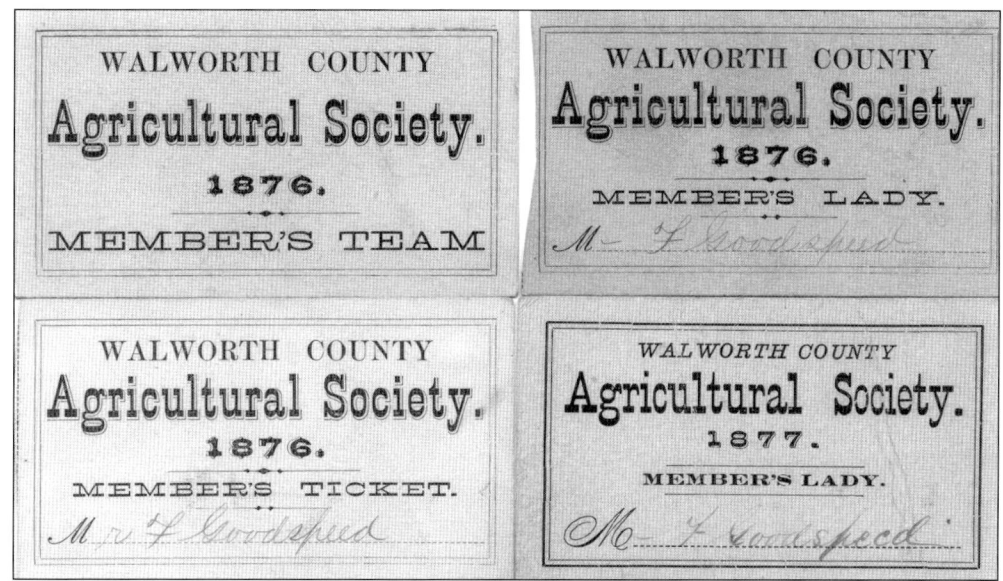

Pictured here are four member tickets for F. Goodspeed dating between 1876 and 1877.

THE CROWNING GLORY.
WALWORTH CO. FAIR
Held at Elkhorn, Wis.

PROGRAMME:

First Day will be devoted to Receiving Entries.

Second Day, Wednesday, September 27, '82.
At 1:30 P.M., Trial of Speed, 2d Divis., or 3-Minute Race. At 2, Bicycle Race; best 2 in 3, ½-mile heats.
WALWORTH CORNET BAND.

Third Day, Thursday, September 28.
At 9 A.M., Examination of Carriage Horses, single and double; also Gent's Driving Horses. At 11, 4th Division, or 2:50 Race. At 1:30 P.M., Trial of Speed in 1st Division, or Stallion Race. At 2:30, 5th Division, or Colt Race.
EAST TROY CORNET BAND.

Fourth Day, Friday, September 29.
At 10:30 A.M., Trial of Speed in 3d Division, 2:35 Race. Between heats best exhibition of Fancy Bicycle Riding. At 1:30 P.M., 6th Division, "Free for All."
WHITEWATER CORNET BAND.

"The Crowning Glory," states this leaflet for the 1882 fair. Notice that the first day is technically reserved for receiving entries to the fair. The next three days are devoted to horse races and appearances by neighboring community cornet bands. The "programme" also lists an exciting bike race Wednesday, September 27. A bike race consisted of the best two of three half-mile heats, an exciting alternative to the other action on the track throughout the fair.

Official fair letterhead dating to 1883 tells Edgar G. Buzzell of Delavan that there will be an official fair officers meeting in Elkhorn on July 8. These days an annual fair board meeting takes place in the depths of winter to review the past fair and to plan for the upcoming one. The meeting is open to all members of the fair board and all season pass holders.

WALWORTH COUNTY Agricultural Society.
Established 1850.
Fair, Sept. 25, 26, 27, 28.

1883.

Elkhorn, Wis.
July 9, 1934.

Mr. Edgar G. Buzzell,
Delavan, Wis.

Dear Edgar:

We will have a meeting of the officers here Wednesday evening July 11th at 8 P.M.

Very truly yours,

Secretary.

Another interesting artistic advertisement, this one for the fair of 1887, shows a man sprouting into a carrot. Or is it a carrot sprouting into a man? Construction for the 1887 building, now the Elkhorn Area School District office, was completed the same year.

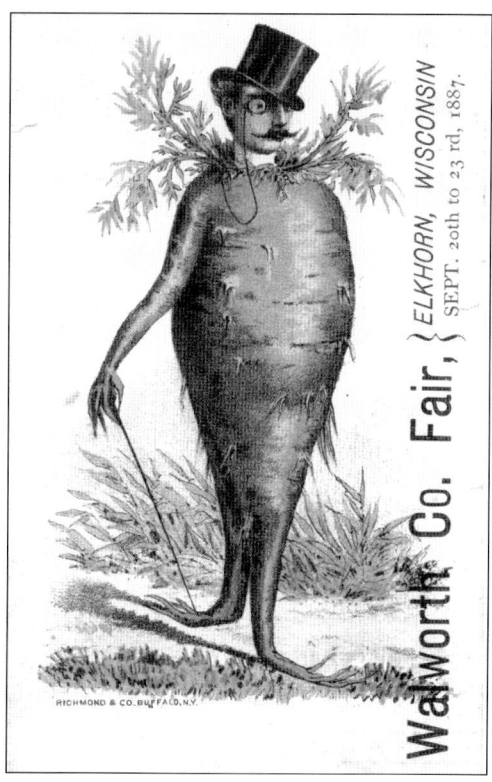

PROGRAMME.

First Day—Tuesday Sept. 20, '87.
Receiving entries and arranging exhibits.

Second Day—Wednesday Sept. 21.
CHILDREN'S DAY.
10:30 A. M......Baby Show. prizes, 1st $25, 2nd $10..
11:00 A. M. ... ...3 year old race, purse $75.
1:30 P. M ... . Stallion Race, purse $150.
2:00 P. M...................2:29 Race, purse $150.
MUSIC—Spring Prairie Cornet Band.

Third Day—Thursday Sept. 22.
Everybody's day—including the Governor and a long list of invited guests.
9:30 A. M............Exhibition of Carriage Horses.
10:30 A. M.............4 year old Race, purse $150.
1:30 P. M...............Pacing Race, purse $100.
2:00 P. M.... ....2:38 Race, purse $150.
MUSIC—Lake Geneva Military Band.

Fourth Day—Friday Sept. 23.
The day when everybody attends to see the races.
9:30 A. M........ Exhibition of Gents' driving horses.
10:00 A. M.....Wedding ceremony in front of Amphitheater, purse $50.
11:00 A. M...................3:00 Race, purse $150.
1:30 P. M.... ....Farmers' Race, purse $100.
2:00 P. M...... ....Free-for-all, purse $250.
MUSIC—Elkhorn Cornet Band and Band Tournament.

RATES OF ADMISSION.
Annual Membership Ticket $1.00
Single Admission Ticket 25
Children's Ticket, between ten and fourteen 10
Double team, one admission, 25 cts., for the week..50
Single horse and rider 50
Supply wagon badges, for team and wagon during the Fair....................................1.00
Tickets can be obtained of the Treasurer for ten days before the Fair.
For any information write the Secretary at Elkhorn Wis.
LEVI E. ALLEN Secretary.

How expensive was it to attend the fair? According to this "programme" from 1887, a full-price adult season pass cost $1. Admission for the day was just 25 cents. Compare that to $8 per day and $25 for a season pass in 2004. Back then the fair only ran three days, with the day before the start reserved for receiving and judging entries.

A European castle adorns a souvenir image advertising the fair of 1888 in late September.

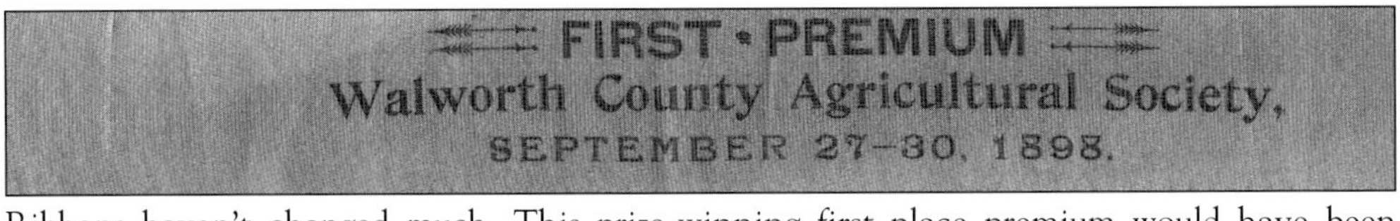

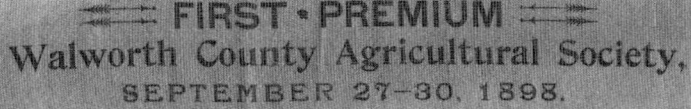

Ribbons haven't changed much. This prize-winning first place premium would have been handed out during the 1888 county fair.

1889
Walworth County Fair.
PROGRAMME.

FIRST DAY—Tuesday, Sept. 24,

Will be devoted to making entries. All entries free to exhibitors, except in Youths' Department, Breeders' Exhibit, Class 12, and Trials of Speed.

PURSES PAID EVERY NIGHT.

SECOND DAY—Wednesday, Sept. 25.

10:00 A. M.,	Base Ball Game and Baby Show.
11:00 "	Stake Race for 2-year-olds and 4-year-old Race.
1:30 P. M.,	Base Ball Game.
2:00 "	Stallion Race.
2:30 "	2:29 Race.

MUSIC, TROY CENTER CORNET BAND.

THIRD DAY—Thursday, Sept. 26.

10:00 A. M.,	Base Ball Game and Exhibition of Carriage Horses.
10:45 "	Stake Race for 3-year-olds.
1:15 P. M.,	Pacing Race and Base Ball Game.
2:15 "	2:38 Race.

MUSIC, SPRING PRAIRIE CORNET BAND.

FOURTH DAY—Friday, Sept. 27.

10:00 A. M.,	Base Ball Game and Exhibition of Gent's Driving Horses.
10:45 "	3:00 Race.
1:15 P. M.,	Farmers' Race and Base Ball Game.
2:15 "	Free-for-All Race.

MUSIC, CORNET BAND FROM WHITEWATER.

THE Society offers a premium for the handsomest baby under the age of one year. Purse, $35.00, divided into five premiums: 1st Premium, $10; 2d, $8; 3d, $7; 4th, $6, and 5th, $4. This exhibition will be upon Children's Day, and held in front of the Amphitheater. Entries in Baby Show to close Tuesday, Sept. 24, 6:00 p.m., and all applications should show name, age, residence, postoffice address, and all parents making entries should obtain from the Secretary's office their entry number and a ribbon and rosette used to designate the little ones competing for the premiums offered.

In trials of speed, entrance fee of 10 per cent in all purses. Entries to close Monday, Sept. 23, at 5 o'clock p.m. Rules of the American Trotting Association to govern.

The Society offers a purse of $100.00 for Base Ball games, divided into 3 premiums: 1st Premium, $50; 2d, $30, and 3d $20. The club winning the most games during the three days of the Fair to take 1st money; the club winning the second in number of games to take 2d money; and the club winning third in number of games to take 3d money.

Address all correspondence with reference to the Fair to

LEVI E. ALLEN, Secretary.

P. O. Address, ELKHORN, Wis.

Baseball games, best-looking baby contests, and harness racing remained the top events according to this program for the fair of 1889. That edition of the fair also featured local cornet bands from Troy Center, Spring Prairie, and Whitewater—all located in Walworth County. One of the most popular events that people watched, besides the marching bands of the parade and horse races, were the baseball games. There was a field set up that fairgoers could view from the grandstand, and the games pitted local towns against each other, for instance, Delavan versus Lake Geneva or Elkhorn against East Troy.

The imagery captured on this poster advertises the 1889 edition of the county fair.

A vintage 1890 print for the fair shows flowers and a little girl. This concept of artistry and advertising continues today, where each year a different theme is given for the fair and carried out in all the print, radio, and website promotions.

Advertisers had their way to attract fairgoers, handing out collectible cards like this one, from the 1890 edition of the county fair. This one could well have been an addition to a scrapbook.

J.M. Grier presided over the fair of 1890, and this was another example of a small card that was handed out to fairgoers advertising the event. The infant inside the basket is most likely not as happy as those who were handed the card.

A girl on a log is greeted by a bird in this souvenir card that was handed out at the fair. There is no date on the card, but it would likely have been used during a fair of the late 1800s.

Yet another fair souvenir card depicts two children out in a field picking flowers.

These guests got into the 1908 Walworth County Fair free with this complimentary pass from the Walworth County Agricultural Society. The fair does maintain a policy that everyone pays to get in, even fair employees.

This ticket, owned by Ezra Peters, appears to be a yearly admission ticket from 1921.

ELKHORN, WIS. Sept. 6 – 10 1926

How long is the fair? It's easy to measure using this ruler that was passed out to visitors in 1926.

33

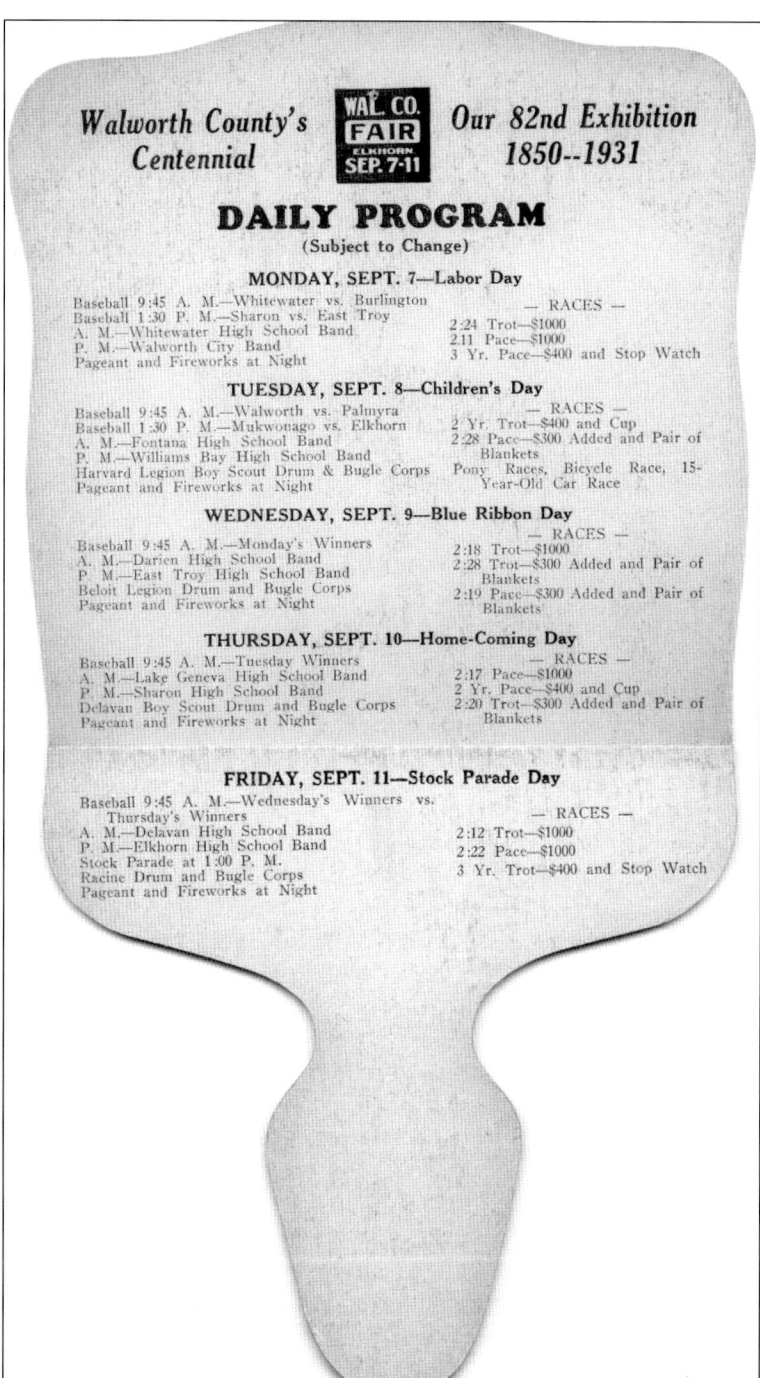

Don't have an umbrella to keep cool? No problem, with this handheld fan given out to fairgoers. Not only did it keep visitors cool, it was also a handy way to check the daily schedule of events. This particular fan listed events in 1931 when the fair had moved to a five-day run.

"The Fair That Always Makes Good" promises the program handed out at the Walworth County Fair of 1932 which ran for five days in early September.

Reserved seating cost a pretty penny in 1934—50 pennies in fact. This ticket was for seat 8E6, good for Thursday afternoon on September 6.

Please Be Kind

Charity becomes less sweet
When someone squawks about his seat!
We'd like to mention it's a task
To please you all just as you ask.

We praise the day that some inventor
Will build a grandstand all dead-center.
In short a place so well designed
There's none in front and none behind.

Be a sport and cause no strife
Position is not all in life.
So have some fun—sit back—relax
And take it off your income tax.

The Walworth County Agricultural Society

"Please Be Kind" and donate to the Walworth County Fair. This advertisement educates fair patrons and potential fair donors about the fact that they can take any donations off their income tax.

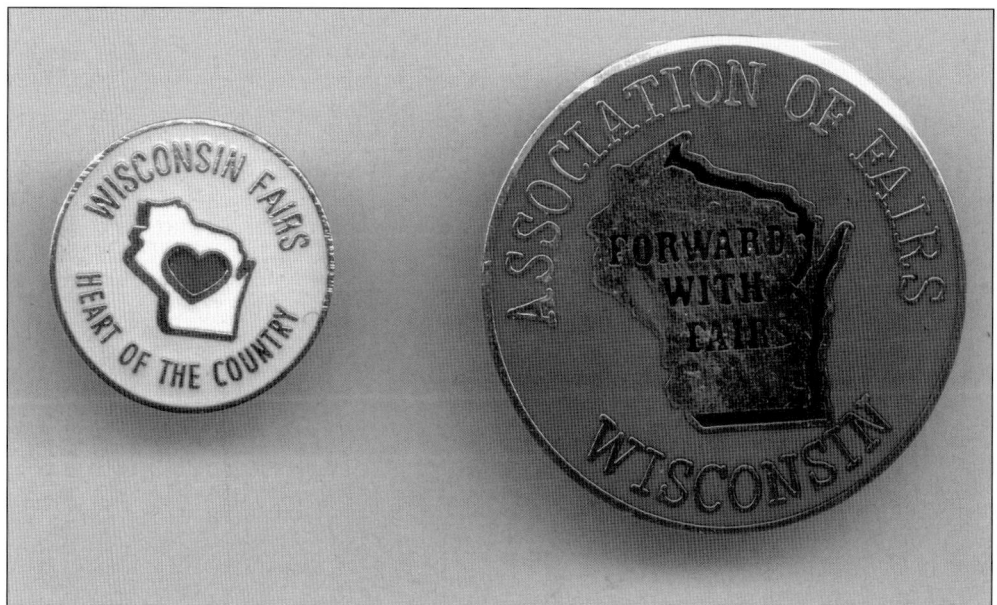

Pictured here is another example of fair memorabilia that has promoted the fair over the years; these two pins display the state of Wisconsin. The pin on the right is from the Wisconsin Association of Fairs and highlights the state motto, "Forward."

Three
PLANES, TRAINS, AND AUTOMOBILES

Finding parking was an issue even at the fair of 1914, as hordes of cars chugged their way to the fairgrounds from all over Walworth County and Southeastern Wisconsin.

This group poses in front of a convertible, showing just how popular the fair had become in the region, drawing visitors from far and wide.

A panoramic view shows the grandstand and vehicles as they begin to pour in and fill the infield of the track to capacity. That same field is still used today and overflows with parking early on the days that there popular concerts.

A row of cars stretches as far as the eye can see as a group of fairgoers pose in front of their vintage wheels at the 1916 fair. Two other people sit inside the automobile to the right, possibly just after pulling into their spot.

Today, blimps hover over major sporting events, and Elkhorn was lucky to receive the Goodyear Blimp. Here, it prepares to make a landing at the fairgrounds.

After the blimp has safely landed, the Goodyear logo is clearly visible on the structure of the craft. About a dozen men attempt to anchor the ship to the ground with ropes.

Using long ropes, this group moors a United States mail plane to the ground at the fair.

A two-seater biplane sits idle; it may be stationed near the largest expanse of field to hold a plane, the track infield. Planes routinely stopped by the fairgrounds to hold aerial acrobatic and stunt shows for enthralled audiences.

Sulkies race by in this photograph captured from the upper deck of the amphitheater. Perhaps many in the audience on this particular day are awaiting the performances of the stunt plane parked on the makeshift tarmac of the infield. Attached to the upper wing is a stand used for the daredevil.

This snapshot taken from high in the grandstand shows a unique event in the history of racing at the fairgrounds. If you look closely, a lone bike racer speeds to the finish in the annual bike race. The bicycle race was an alternative to the horse racing, and when the biker had turned in two laps, he would have gone one mile. Fans lean over the infield railings to cheer him on.

Activity fills the grounds even when the fair is not running. Stables are full, and trotting takes place on the track throughout the summer and fall. This scene shows a carriage posing at the finish line of the track with an eerily empty grandstand.

Pictured here is one of the trains that brought visitors to the fair. The Eagle Line was the spur of railroad that headed to the fair with visitors each day during the fair's run. They came from destinations like Milwaukee, Madison, and Janesville.

Special Excursion Trains to Walworth County Fair
ELKHORN, WIS., SEPT. 20, 21, 22, 23, 1910.

ARRIVE	TIME OF ARRIVAL AT AND DEPARTURE FROM FAIR GROUNDS.	DEPART
10:10 a.m.	Libertyville (Thursday and Friday)..............	5:35 p.m.
9:05 a.m.	Walworth (Thursday only).......................	6:15 p.m.
8:50 a.m.	Janesville (Thursday and Friday)................	6:15 p.m.
10:25 a.m.	Freeport (Thursday only).........................	5:00 p.m.
9:55 a.m.	Beloit (Wednesday, Thursday, Friday)..........	5:50 p.m.
9:55 a.m.	Rockford (Thursday)..............................	5:50 p.m.
9:21 a.m.	Madison (Wednesday, Thursday, Friday)......	4:55 p.m.
9:21 a.m.	Waukesha (Wednesday, Thursday, Friday)..	4:55 p.m.
9:30 a.m.	Racine (Wednesday, Thursday, Friday)........	5:20 p.m.

REGULAR TRAINS LEAVE ELKHORN STATION

East: 7:03 a.m. / 1:17 p.m. / 6:19 p.m.

West: 10:53 a.m. / 2:10 p.m. / 5:23 p.m.

Trains have had an important history in the shaping of the county fair. Nineteen special trains from all over southeastern Wisconsin and northern Illinois would shepherd passengers to the fairgrounds. This schedule highlights the train times for the four day run of the fair in 1910.

NINETEEN EXCURSION TRAINS TO THE WALWORTH COUNTY FAIR, AT ELKHORN, WISCONSIN, SEP. 21, 22, 23, 24, 1915.

The Chicago, Milwaukee & St. Paul Railway, in addition to its six regular trains, run nineteen Special Trains to Walworth County Fair, which unload at the Fair Grounds.

The trains start from Libertyville, Rockford, Savanna, Walworth, Beloit, Madison, Janesville, Milwaukee, Racine and Waukesha, stopping at all intermediate points.

All Special Train leave the Fair Grounds each evening after the Races.

Nineteen excursion trains devoted their service to the Walworth County Fair. For over a hundred years, people have known about the fair that turns Elkhorn into a metropolis each summer. In 1915, fairgoers used this placard as a way to find out when the trains were headed to the station at the fairgrounds. Perhaps the widespread tradition of the fair's popularity with people all over the Midwest was started when families took the tracks to the fair and passed their love of the annual jaunt down through the generations.

It may be different in style and productivity, but the concept of the tractor like this one and the farm machinery display has not changed although the impact of farming and updates in technology have led to bigger tractors. Because of that, the Walworth County Fair now boasts the largest farm machinery display in the Midwest.

Here farm machinery operates the way it used to near a large pile of hay.

Three Elkhorn youth bicycle out of the fairgrounds under the main gate. Beyond the gate, from left to right, are: the dining hall, the Educational Department, Horticulture, 4-H Clubs, the cream puff and éclair building, and the Treasurer's Office with restrooms on the lower floors. Most of these buildings, which comprised "Dining Hall Row" in the early 1900s, are still standing today.

Claire Doane shows that work must be done even during the off-season. He has worked at the fair since high school and is still employed there today. The barn in the upper corner of the photograph has been replaced with the North Activities Building where commercial booths set up shop and a wing is devoted to food judging.

Four
POSTCARDS

Above is a view of the midway from one of the earliest postcards that was created for the Walworth County Fair in 1909.

WALWORTH COUNTY FAIR, SEPT. 20-23, 1910, ELKHORN, WIS.

A sea of fairgoers streams through "Dining Hall Row." The building at the very far end is the grandstand.

Amphitheater at the Great Walworth County Fair, Elkhorn, Wis.
(LONGEST IN THE WORLD, ON A 1-2 MILE TRACK.)
Sept. 20 - 21 - 22 - 23 - 1910

World records at the county fair in Elkhorn are nothing new, and this postcard accentuates that the amphitheater, set along a half-mile oval track, was the longest in the world. The postcard shows the 1910 fair.

Midway at the Great Walworth County Fair, Elkhorn, Wis. Sept. 20-21-22-23-1910

The grandstand looms in the background of the midway in this postcard image, also from 1910.

WALWORTH COUNTY FAIR, SEPT. 20-23, 1910, ELKHORN, WIS.

This postcard view is from the southern end of the grandstand. Over the years, postcards have become a popular way to showcase the fair, and this one has forever captured the trackside view from the fair of 1910.

WALWORTH COUNTY FAIR. SEPT. 20-23, 1910. ELKHORN, WIS.

Horses and people share the track during some downtime, as shown on a postcard for the 1910 county fair held September 20–23.

The Great Walworth County Fair at Elkhorn, Wis., Sept. 7-8-9-10, 1920.

Longtime Marshal George Wylie stands guard in front of the old grandstand. Wylie was also a member of government at the county level, as well as a sheriff.

"Along the Pike." Visit the Walworth County Fair, Elkhorn, Wis. Sept. 19—22, 1

"Along the Pike" in this 1911 postcard shows hundreds of visitors walking past sideshows and food booths with the Ferris wheel in the center.

"Dining Hall Row." Visit the Walworth County Fair, Elkhorn, Wis. Sept. 19—22, 1911

"Visit the Walworth County Fair on Sept. 19–22, 1911" invites this postcard picture of the famous Dining Hall Row.

**Down the Midway, Walworth County Fair, Elkhorn, Wis.
Visit the Fair, Sept. 17-18-19-20—1912.**

"Down the Midway" a Ferris wheel dominates the fairgrounds, towering above the grandstand and tents. This postcard dates back to 1912.

"Filled to the Gates," Walworth County Fair Grounds, Elkhorn, Wis. Visit the Fair, Sept. 16-17-18-19, 1913.

This 1913 postcard captures the enormous crowds that spilled through the main gates at the fair. The view looks toward what are currently Highway 11 and the large main parking lot.

Automobile Grounds, Walworth County Fair, Elkhorn, Wis.
Visit the Fair, Sept. 16-17-18-19, 1913.

By 1913, the Walworth County Fair had become so popular that an entire field was devoted to the cars that ventured from across the countryside to attend the event.

The Great Fair at Elkhorn, Wis., Sept. 19-20-21-22, 1916.

Two men discuss judging of horses in an open-air arena at the Walworth County Fair of 1916. Crowds stand rather than sit at this particular stage of judging. The building in the background may be the stable where these horses were housed through the duration of the fair.

Automobile Grounds, Walworth County Fair, Elkhorn, Wis. Sept. 17-18-19-20, 1918.

The very idea of the Walworth County Fair, even in 1918, conjured up images of the countryside, although the popularity caused increased crowds, and those in cars had to brave the same parking issues that occur today.

"The Finish," The Great Walworth County Fair at Elkhorn, Wis., Sept. 16-17-18-19, 1919.

Overflow crowds spill out of the grandstand near the rails of the track while the horses blaze past to the finish line. This image was emblazoned on a postcard from the fair held in mid-September of 1919.

"On the Midway," The Great Walworth County Fair at Elkhorn, Wis., Sept. 16-17-18-19, 1919.

The midway today is vastly different than it was in this postcard from 1919. Though the high-tech rides, neon lights, and carnival games did not yet exist, legions of fans attended and packed the midway.

The Great Walworth County Fair at Elkhorn, Wis., Sept. 7-8-9-10, 1920.

A postcard declaring, "The Great Walworth County Fair," shows a view of the old grandstand packed with people from end to end. The longtime head of the fair, George Wylie, stands guard, with his horse, on the track.

The original stock pavilion in this postcard from 1920 was one of the finest buildings of its kind at the time.

Pictured here is an envelope celebrating 120 years of the Walworth County Fair with a cachet of a harness racer on the left portion. The cancellation on the stamp shows that this letter was mailed out of Elkhorn in 1970.

The front side of the same envelope shows there is no shortage of methods employed by the Walworth County Agricultural Society to spread the word of the fair throughout the countryside. This envelope advertises the 1882 installment of the fair, which ran four days in late September.

In 1939, the log cabin located in the park at the fairgrounds was transformed to fit the theme of a Juneau trading post of 1820. These days, the cabin displays a famous, long-running exhibit that asks fairgoers to guess the importance of odd and little-known objects.

Five
JUDGEMENT DAY

A well-placed camera captures the two-horse team pulling a wagon as it rides past spectators and judges. The stock pavilion was the precursor to the Wiswell Center, the current location for the Meat Animal Sale at the fair's end; it is visible in the background.

The same team is handled by judges as they inspect horses and carriage in order to decide who gets the coveted awards and subsequent bragging rights until the next year's fair.

> William Rasch, local meat and grocery man, has purchased two beeves which took first prizes at the Walworth county and Zenda fairs last summer. These cattle were raised by 4-H club members.
> Mr. Rasch gives Clifford and Donald Snudden credit for raising the finest beeves ever [ ] Lake Geneva.

Two local boys, Clifford and Donald Snudden, pose with their prize beeves, which won first place honors at both the Walworth County and Zenda Fairs.

(left) This award, presented by the Wisconsin Horse Breeders Association, was given to the best foal by a pure-bred draft sire; it signified a paycheck and recognition at the Walworth County Fair of 1912.

(above) The fruits of labor are rewarded with shiny ribbons of all colors. Pictured, from left to right, are: a third premium award from 1910, a second premium ribbon from 1902, and a first premium award handed out during the fair of 1939.

A group of young men show their sheepskin exhibitions to a judge at the north end of the sheep barn in the late 1930s. Pictured, from left to right, are: Bell Thayer, Harold Lundt, Elmer Lundt, Robert Thayer, Ken Disch, unidentified, Clarence Potter, and Bill Duncan (judge).

An official judge's ribbon is all that identifies this woman as she peeks through the entries of pumpkins, squash, and tomatoes. The food judging events at the fair have long held appeal to local citizens who prepare recipes for bread and cakes long before the Labor Day weekend arrives in anticipation that their recipe will be crowned the best.

A jar of apples gets scrutinized and critiqued by a judge.

Walworth County Agricultural Society

SECRETARY'S OFFICE,

Little Prairie, Wis., April 22, 1878.

SIDNEY BUELL, President,
BLOOMFIELD.

H. G. HOLLISTER, Vice-Pres.
DELAVAN.

HOLLIS LATHAM, Treas.
ELKHORN.

$3,500 In Premiums Given Away. Competition Open to the World.

Farmers Plant for the Coming Fair, To be Held at Elkhorn, Sep. 24, 25, 26 and 27.

Send for List to W. H. MORRISON, Little Prairie, Wis.

CLASS 16—FARM PRODUCTS.
(Cereals.)

JUDGES.—C. K. Phelps, Ch'n, Geneva; J. R. Kling, Troy; Andrew Johnson, Whitewater. Umpire—C. L. Douglas, Walworth.

Best bushel Spring Wheat	$2 00
Second best,	2 00
Third best,	1 00
Best bushel of Rye	2 00
Second best,	1 00
Best bushel of Barley	2 00
Second best,	1 00
Best bushel Yellow Dent Corn	3 00
Second best,	2 00
Third best,	1 00
Best bushel White Dent Corn	2 00
Second best,	1 00
Best bushel Flint Corn	2 00
Second best,	1 00
Best bushel Beans	1 00
Best bushel of Peas	1 00
Second best,	1 00
Best bushel of Clover Seed	2 00
Second best,	1 00
Best bushel of Timothy	2 00
Second best,	1 00
Best bushel of Flax seed	2 00
Second best,	1 00
Best bushel of Hungarian seed	1 00
Best bushel of Millet seed	1 00
Best bushel of white Oats	2 00
Second best,	1 00
Best bushel of black Oats	2 00
Second best,	1 00
Best show of cereals	8 00
Second best,	5 00
Best sample of Broom Corn	1 00
Best sample of Hops	00

CLASS 17—FARM PRODUCTS.
[Judges same as for Class 16.]
(Vegetables.)

Best half bushel of Potatoes	$2 00
Second best,	1 00
Best half bushel of Table Beets	2 00
Second best,	1 00
Best half bushel of Field Beets	2 00
Second best,	1 00
Best half bushel of Onions	2 00
Second best,	1 00
Best Carrots	2 00
Second best,	1 00
Best Parsnips	2 00
Second best,	1 00

Best Cabbages, three in number	2 00
Second best,	1 00
Best Cauliflowers, three in number	2 00
Second best,	1 00
Best Brocoli, three in number	2 00
Second best,	1 00
Best Field Squash	
Second best,	1 00
Best Table Squash	2 00
Second best,	1 00
Best show Cucumbers	2 00
Second best,	1 00
Best Pumpkins, three in number	2 00
Second best,	1 00
Best Turnips, six in number	2 00
Second best,	1 00
Best peck of Sweet Potatoes	2 00
Second best,	1 00
Best Tomatoes, twelve in number	1 00
Second best,	50
Best sample of Sweet Corn	1 00
Second best,	50
Best Water Melons, three in number	1 00
Second best,	50
Best Musk Melons, three in number	1 00
Second best,	50

CLASS 25—BOY'S DEPARTMENT.
(Garden Products.)

Best Specimen Potatoes, half bushel	$1 00
Second best,	50
Best Specimen Onions	1 00
Second best,	50
Best Exhibition Beets	1 00
Second best,	50
Best Sample Tomatoes, twelve in number	1 00
Second best,	50
Best Sample Pop Corn	1 00
Second best,	50
Best variety of Garden Products	3 00
Second best,	2 00
Third best	1 00
Best Bouquet Cut Flowers	2 00
Second best,	1 00

CLASS 28—FLOWERS AND PLANTS.

JUDGES.—Edward Balsley, Ch'n, LaFayette; Mrs. H. A. Congar, Whitewater; Mrs. D. L. Flack, Geneva.

UMPIRE.—Mrs. Harley Sanford, LaGrange.

Best and most artistically arranged Floral Design	$2 00
Best and most tastefully arranged collection of Cut Flowers	1 00
Second best,	1 00
Best and most tastefully arranged Basket of Flowers	2 00
Second best,	1 00
Best Pyramidal Bouquet	2 00
Best pair Round Bouquets	2 00
Second best,	1 00
Best pair Flat Bouquets, in sand or water	2 00
Second best,	1 00
Best Bouquet of Everlasting Flowers	2 00
Second best,	1 00
Best collection of Dahlias	2 00
Second best,	1 00
Best collection of Roses	2 00
Second best,	1 00
Best collection of Perenial Phlox	1 00
Second best,	50
Best collection of Gladiolus	1 00
Second best,	50
Best collection of Tube Roses	1 00
Second best,	50
Best collection of Lilies	1 00
Second best,	50
Best Hanging Basket with Plants	1 00
Second best,	50
Best Smilax on trellis	1 00
Best collection of Anterrhinum	1 00
Second best,	50
Best collection of Asters	1 00
Second best,	50
Best collection of Verbenas	1 00
Second best,	50
Best collection of Pansies	1 00
Second best,	50
Best collection of Double Petunias	1 00
" " Single	1 00
Best collection of Phlox Drummondii	1 00
Second best,	50
Best collection of Stocks	1 00
Second best,	50
Best collection of Balsams	1 00
Second best,	50
Best collection of House Plants, not less than 25 or more than 50 varieties	5 00
Second best,	3 00
Best 10 Geraniums	2 00
Second best,	1 00
Best 6 Fuchsias	2 00
Second best,	1 00
Best 6 Carnations	2 00
Second best,	1 00
Best collection Ornamental Foliage Plants	2 00
Second best,	1 00

SPECIAL PREMIUM,

Offered by James Vick, Seedsman & Florist, Rochester, N. Y.

Best collection Cut Flowers—A Flower Chromo.

The first place best bushel of rye paid $2.00 according to the premium chart from the 1878 Walworth County Fair. Sidney Buell from Bloomfield Township was president of the fair that year.

The silo of the old stock pavilion rises above a booth selling farm equipment. The scene inside the old stock pavilion, the new Wiswell building, is the culmination of judging at the annual Meat Animal Sale during which top bidders purchase prize animals.

Six
Time for a Parade

A young man shows his beauty in front of the grandstand while another man tries to wrangle two horses behind him. This artist rendering served as a poster for the 1891 Walworth County Fair that ran from September 22 through September 25.

Before the days of spectator sports, the stock parade at the county fair set a tradition of excitement and a variety of interesting animals competing in front of both judges and audience.

FRIDAY
Stock Parade Day

Program September 9th

9:00 A. M.—Spelling Contest—Stock Pavilion.
9:00 A. M.—Delavan High School Band.
9:45 A. M.—Baseball—Wednesday's Winners vs. Thursday's Winners.
1:00 P. M.—Walworth High School Band.
1:00 P. M.—Concert—Holton-Elkhorn Band.
1:15 P. M.—Stock Parade.
1:30 P. M.—Races Called.
4:00 P. M.—Pig Contest.
7:00 P. M.—Concert.
7:30 P. M.—Attractions.
8:00 P. M.—Revue and Wedding.

Speed Program

2:20 Pace—$1000 (Early Closing Event)
Free for All Trot—$400 (Late Closing Event)
3 yr. Trot—$400 and Stop Watch (Early Closing Event)

Whitewater Press Print

Pictured here is a daily list of activities for Friday, "Stock Parade Day" at the fair, from a fair program. Included are concerts from local bands, the actual stock parade at midday, a baseball game, and a pig contest, which is shown in the drawing on the program.

Local farmers parade their prize cows in front of judges and audience in hope of winning ribbons.

A child's head pokes above the frame of the picture while a man leads his horse in the stock parade of 1911.

The track is filled with cows led in all different directions while a captivated audience peers on from both the grandstand (where the photographer is stationed) and the infield.

By the looks of the late-1960s era car heading south on the track, this is one of the last stock parades in front of the amphitheater at the fairgrounds before it was destroyed by fire.

A crowd of white dress shirts and ties fills the original amphitheater as the stock parade passes on the track. The men on the field appear to be leading cows.

No seatbelt laws are in effect as slow-moving trailer beds full of standing young men navigate through the stock parade on the track. This truck is from local Borg Farms.

A tractor pulls a wagon advertising Potters Sheep in the stock parade. Poking above the cowboy hats in the trailer is the fence for the baseball field in the middle of the track.

Long before cars were decorated with streamers and filled with passengers tossing out candy at parades, horses pulling buggies signaled the opening of each annual fair. This buggy is decorated with flowers and the dates of that year's fair in mid-September.

THE BEST OF ALL!
WALWORTH COUNTY FAIR,
ELK HORN, WIS.

PROGRAM:
First Day—Receiving Entries.

Second Day—WEDNESDAY, SEPT. 26, 1883.
TRIAL OF SPEED, DIV. 4.

The 2.50 Race at 10-30 and RUNNING RACE at 11 A. M. *Wednesday Afternoon*—DIV. 1. Free for all Stallions.

ELK HORN CORNET BAND.

Third Day—THURSDAY, SEPT. 27.

At 9-30 A. M. Exhibition of Carriage Horses—Single and Double, and Trial of Speed, Div. 5.
At 1-30 P. M. Div. 3, or 2.35 Race.
At 2 P. M. Div. 2, or 3 minute Race.

WHITEWATER CORNET BAND.

Fourth Day—FRIDAY, SEPT. 28.

At 9-30 A. M. Exhibition of Gents.' Driving Horses.
At 10-30 A. M. WALWORTH COUNTY Race.
At 1-30 P. M. Div. 6,—Free for all Trotters.

DELAVAN CORNET BAND.

—COME TO THE FAIR—

W. H. MORRISON, Sec'y.   ORRIS PRATT, Pres't.

Prof. Horsford's Phosphatic Baking Powder

is the best, strongest and healthiest baking powder made. It is recommended by leading physicians, and makes lighter bread, biscuit and cakes than any other powder.

FOR SALE BY ALL GROCERS.

"The best of all," proclaims a leaflet for the 1883 fair. This fair lasted only three days, occurring before the board upped the length of the fair to four days. The major entertainment, according to this paper, is showings by the Elkhorn, Whitewater, and Delavan Cornet Bands.

In addition to the stock parade at the end of the fair, a festive parade marked the beginning of the fair when groups like the Racine Cornet Band made an appearance on the track. In the early years of the fair, many local cornet bands played in front of crowds at the fairgrounds amphitheater and on stages throughout the grounds.

A band from East Troy marches down the track in front of a bunch of children holding a banner that proclaims, "Youth Marches Forward," during the stock parade.

A farm truck gets dressed up for the parade that signifies the opening of the fair each year.

Even elected officials used the parade as a way to peddle votes; the only difference from today is that they didn't have convertibles. Burkett and his decorated carriage ride past with a sign to inform fairgoers he is running for Congress.

Another procession that no longer exists was the vintage car parade that wound its way through the fairgrounds. Here, Tom Amon of Elkhorn prepares to drive his vintage DeSoto. The parade began at the northeastern gate near the power plant and headed to the fairgrounds, the park stage, and out through the Armory Gate.

Tom Amon's car makes it way down one of the streets of the fairgrounds under the watchful eyes of enthralled spectators.

Seven
Harnessing a Tradition

A high-wheeled sulky races neck and neck with the competition toward the finish line while the infield crowd cheers. The scene is immortalized on this Walworth County Fair flyer from 1891.

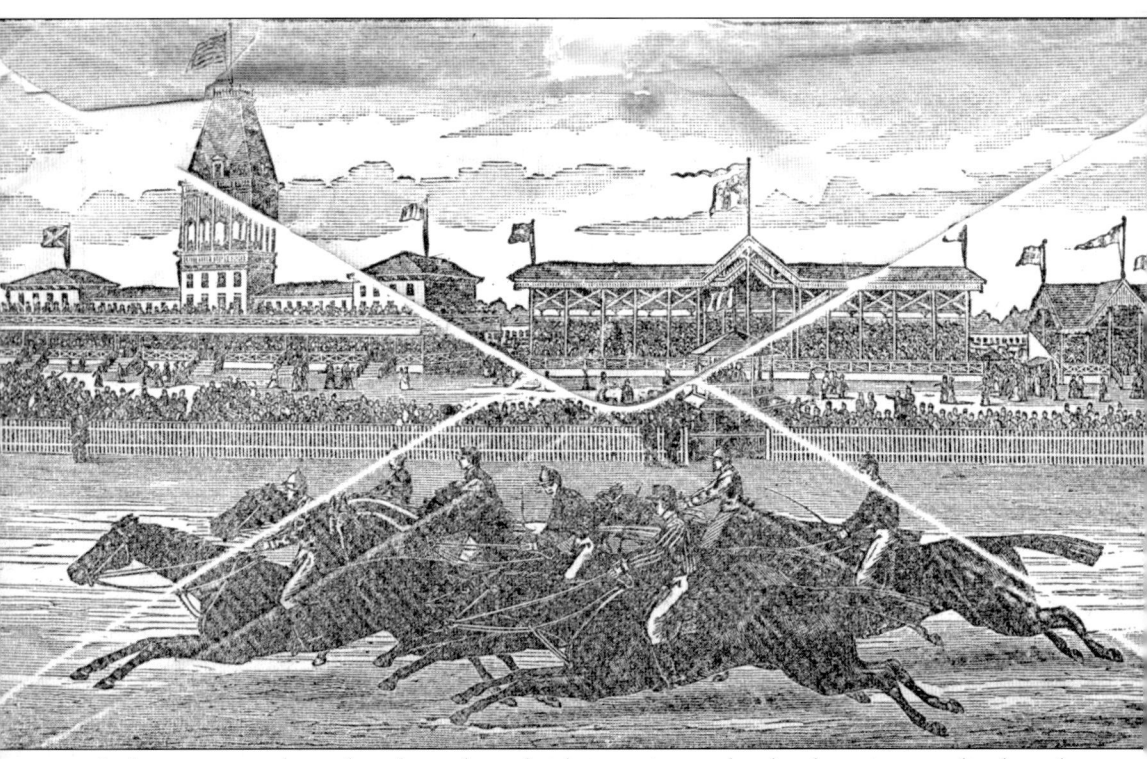

Jockeys position themselves for a photo finish in an image that has been immortalized on the back of this envelope. The event depicted here was also featured in the fair program handed out for the 1882 fair.

Harness racers three-wide speed down the track to reach the finish line while onlookers watch the action from the infield.

The pacer horse gallops to the finish in record time. All four of the pacer's feet are off the ground as he finishes in two minutes and sixteen seconds, breaking his previous records. The race took place September 19, 1918.

"Number Five" crosses the finish line in the third and final heat trot on September 19, 1918. The tower at the finish line is plastered with advertising of sponsors of the fair and races. On the very top, an ad proclaims that Walworth County's favorite newspaper is the *Elkhorn Independent*.

A horse is led into an open field near one of the fairgrounds stables.

These long horse barns were located at the far northeastern corner of the fairgrounds. They were packed most of the year from the start of the fair through the off-season in fall and spring. It is still not uncommon to see horses and their trainers racing the track on a cool October morning.

Walworth County Agricultural Society

TRIALS OF SPEED.
1891.

— PROGRAM —

Wednesday, Sept. 23d.

2:50 TROTTING	Purse,	$350 00
STALLION RACE,	"	350 00

Thursday, Sept. 24th.

2:30 PACING RACE,	Purse,	$400 00
2:29 TROTTING,	"	400 00

Friday, Sept. 25th.

2:40 TROTTING,	Purse,	$350 00
FREE-FOR-ALL,	"	500 00

SUBJECT TO CONDITIONS OF SOCIETY:

Purses paid at end of each race. Entrance fee 10 per cent in all purses. Four to enter, three to start, unless otherwise mentioned.

ENTRIES CLOSE SEPT. 15TH.

Good Track. Good Stables. A good time. For further particulars address,

W. J. STRATTON, SECY.

ELKHORN, WIS.

Trials of Speed at the fair of 1891 paid a pretty penny for the winners. This sample program was handed out to spectators over the three days of racing that year. The most lucrative race was the finale on Friday, September 25, which paid a hefty $500 to the winner.

Before the advent of timing technology, volunteers kept track of the time and winners of harness race heats. This ribbon was handed out during the fair of 1920.

Horses standing in the infield watch horses of a completely different pedigree racing out on the track in the early years of the fair.

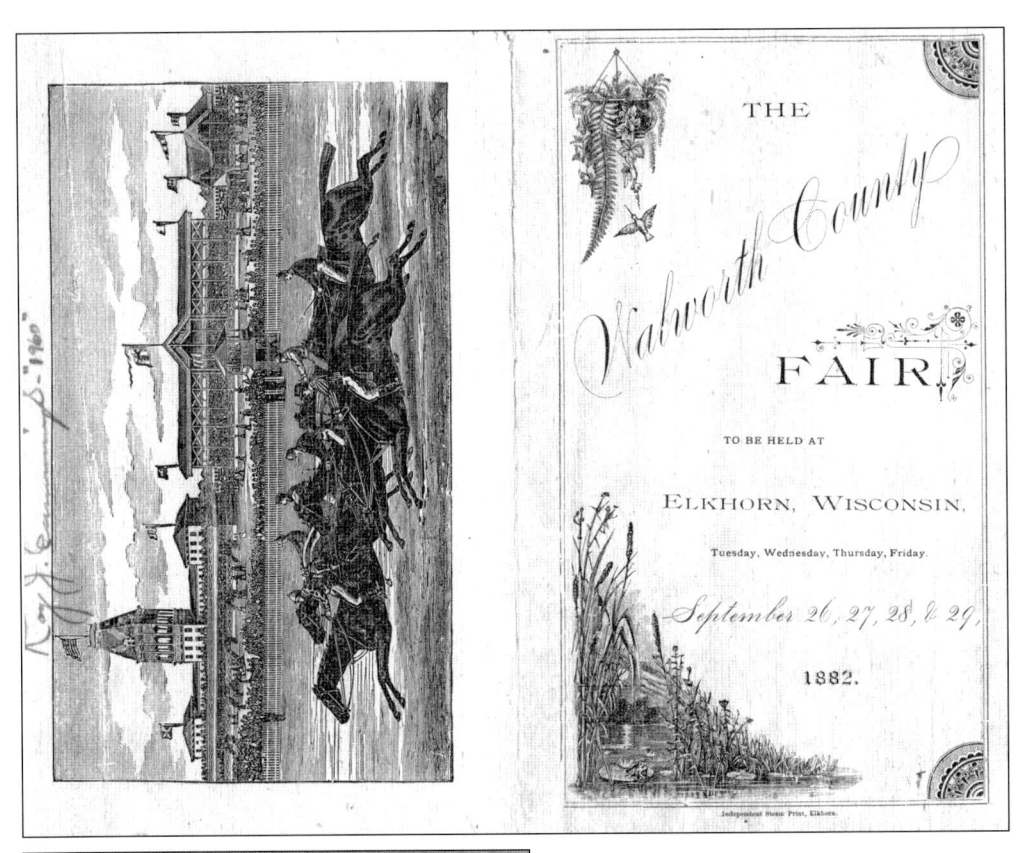

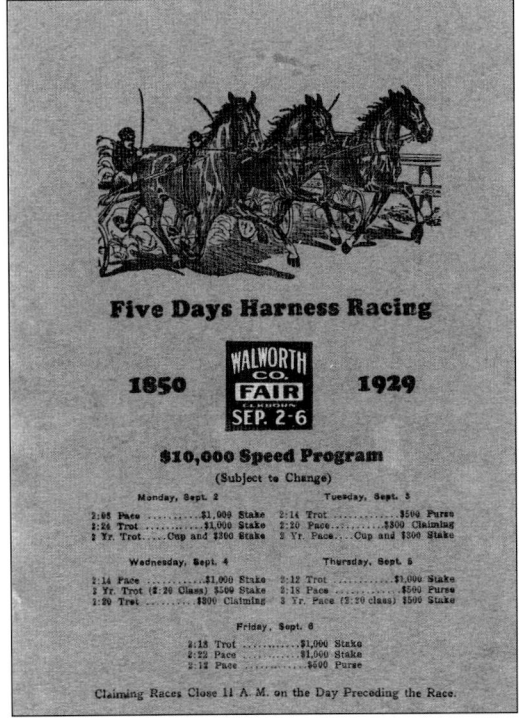

(*above*) Decorative artwork graced the cover and backside of the harness racing program of 1882. The images of a large stadium and jockeys on horseback conjure up thoughts of the great racing in Kentucky.

(*left*) Five days of horse racing in 1929 boasted a speed program worth more than $10,000. That alone was enough to draw strong crowds and harness racers from across the Midwest.

Walworth County Agricultural Society.

THE BIGGEST COUNTY FAIR IN THE UNITED STATES,

Held at ELKHORN, WIS.

Sept. 24, 25, 26 and 27, 1895.

$5,000 IN PREMIUMS.

Speed Department $2,750.

DON'T MISS THE GREAT FAIR,

J. G. MEADOWS, President.   S. MITCHELL, Secretary.

CALVERT LITH. CO., DETROIT

During the "Great Fair of 1895," the Walworth County Fair reached its zenith, known as the biggest in the entire United States.

Trials of Speed.

Class 31.

Judges will be chosen each day of the Fair by the Executive Committee.

FIRST DIVISION.

Free for all Stallions. Purse, $100.00. Four to enter, and three to go. Mile heats, in harness—best two in three. Time required, 2:50. Stallions to have been kept in service the past season.

First horse	$50 00
Second horse	35 00
Third horse	15 00

SECOND DIVISION.

Free for all horses that have never beaten 3 minutes. No. 2. Purse, $80.00.

First horse	$50 00
Second horse	25 00
Third horse	10 00

THIRD DIVISION.

Free for all horses that have 2:35. No. 3. Purse, $145.00.

First horse	$75 00
Second horse	40 00
Third horse	30 00

FOURTH DIVISION.

Free for all horses that never beat 2:50. No. 4. Purse, $95.00.

First horse	$50 00
Second horse	30 00
Third horse	15 00

FIFTH DIVISION.

Free for all colts 4 years and under. No. 5. Purse, $35.00.

First horse	$20 00
Second horse	10 00
Third horse	5 00

There were a total of six racing divisions in which stallions competed for free. Races were broken down into the best two of three harness heats for a mile, meaning spectators got to see the racers speed by two full laps on the track.

Today, the fair still pays out premiums to the top contestants in animal and food judging, as well as for winners in the demolition derby. Over a hundred years ago, the cash payouts were big for competing horse racers, and this program shows that first place winners in the sixth division received a handsome $150. Those with questions regarding rules or purses were asked to speak to fair secretary, W.H. Morrison.

Speakers have been added to the track to announce the action. Horse racers at the fairgrounds in Elkhorn run on one of the fastest half-mile tracks in the Midwest.

First place is only two turns away and it appears to be a tight race. Horse racing was a main factor in the high attendance levels at the fair for many years and is still relatively popular today, though not as much as in its heyday. The new grandstand figures prominently in the background of the photograph, packed with people.

For a perspective in how far horse racing has come at the fairgrounds, one only needs to reflect on this image of a high-wheeled sulky racing along at breakneck speeds. The greater speeds afforded to the racer by the sulky led it to quickly become the favored form of racing in the mid-nineteenth century. It comprised a straight iron axle and five-diameter wheels, with the total package weighing in around 100 pounds.

Flash forward to the late 1960s and one of the last races in front of the grand amphitheater. A late model car outfitted with gates puts the horses in a trotting position, allowing them to get a quick start to the race.

Shown here is the southwestern turn with the view of the modern-day grandstand in the background. Though harness racing has a long history at the Walworth County Fair, the sport is not as popular as it used to be, and it is difficult to pull together lucrative purses and draw racers from south of Wisconsin.

Eight
LIVE IN CONCERT

Thousands pack the grandstand and track seating to see Johnny Cash perform alongside his wife and fellow country musician, June Carter Cash. That Saturday fair attendance set a record, with 40,961 people, making it one of the largest concerts ever at the fairgrounds.

Anyone who was anyone was at the fair grandstand seeing one of two "big free" shows by the Osmond Brothers on Sunday, September 1. Even though the fair has begun on a variety of dates—most of them in late September—the fair is now held each Labor Day weekend, and signifies the end to summer.

The Fabulous Osmond Brothers
Sunday, Sept. 1 — 2 Big Free Shows, 6:00 and 8:00 P. M.

Randy Travis is surrounded by fair personnel. Pictured here, from left to right, are Duane "Skip" Katzman, fair vice-president; Norman Meyer, fair president; Judy Vance, fair secretary; Randy Travis; and Jimmy Jay, whose company ran the grandstand shows. Travis is just one of hundreds of country celebrities who have played to crowds at the Walworth County Fair. With the advent of the new grandstand and seating on the track, artists could play to more than ten thousand fans. With two shows a night in years past, someone like Randy Travis could play to more than twenty-thousand fans in a single evening.

With the popularity of *American Idol* on television, the fair has found its own way to boost attendance through the creation of the "Country Idol" contest. With support and backing from community businesses, contestants sing their favorite country song, and the winner is judged by the audience at the Park Stage on the fairgrounds. The winner receives a once-in-a-lifetime opportunity to open for one of the country acts, singing on stage in front of thousands. Here, the first Country Idol, David Wayne Marshall, poses.

Country Idol winner David Wayne Marshall performs his song in front of the more than fifteen-thousand fans jamming into the grandstand to hear Australian breakout country singer, Keith Urban, who performed at the fair in 2004.

Next up after Marshall was Keith Urban, who peppered his concert with engaging stories of a girlfriend who lived in Madison and of his road trip to Milwaukee on a Harley.

Randy Travis reprised his past visits with an encore performance to enthusiastic fans, also in 2004.

Nine
CHANGING TIMES

Walworth County Agricultural Society.
The Greatest County Fair in United States.
Held at ELKHORN, WIS.,
Sept. 29 & 30 and Oct 1 & 2, 1896
A new HALF MILE REGULATION TRACK, one of the best in the Northwest.
A new AMPHITHEATER with seating capacity for FOUR THOUSAND PEOPLE.
DON'T MISS THE GREAT FAIR.
J. M. BREWSTER, Pres   SAMUEL MITCHELL, Sec'y.

The year 1896 marked the inauguration of the new amphitheater grandstand, which had the capacity to seat four-thousand people. "Don't Miss the Great Fair," states this card that reminded citizens of the dates of the fair: September 29 & 30 and October 1 & 2. The ad also claims that the track was one of the best in the entire Northwest, a telling sign of the popularity of the fair and the geography of the day.

Pictured here is an aerial shot which accompanied a newspaper article that shows the layout of the grounds around 1930. A lot has changed since this photograph was taken; the grandstand burned down and fire has also claimed a horse barn, as well as the large Floral Hall that occupied a large chunk of what is currently the midway. Cattle barns were replaced after a significant snowfall destroyed the roofs.

This image captures a tragic day in the history of the fairgrounds. An Elkhorn boy watches from the field that occupies the midway as a fire consumes the last remaining timbers of the wooden amphitheater on July 25, 1970. Arson was suspected, but never was proved. Because the fair was a few months away, football bleachers were used for trackside seating and a replacement grandstand was built in 1971.

"Did You Donate?" questions a sticker handed out to donors of Walworth County. When the original and much beloved grandstand burned down in 1970, the Walworth County Agricultural Society offered incentives such as this sticker to those who contributed to a fund helping to rebuild a new grandstand.

Perhaps the most tragic moment in the fair's history came on November 30, 1975, when fire engulfed and destroyed one of the horse stables. Elkhorn Volunteer Fire Department crews battle the fire on the main front in bitter cold weather as thick black smoke billows into the sky. Groom George Anderson and 26 harness race horses lost their lives in the fire.

Above is an aerial view of the way things used to look at the county fairgrounds. New horse barns are located alongside Highway 11, and the open-air arena in the lower corner no longer exists. In this photo, the grandstand would have been in its infancy.

Construction progresses on the new finish-line tower that rises directly next to the new stage where country and rock acts appear. The tower serves as a post to call the action of the tractor pulls and horse racing, but also as a place for fair dignitaries and those with backstage passes to catch the tunes of a nightly concert.

In this image, rain has delayed the construction on the tower in its early stages. The top of the old tower that stood watch over the track for many years has been dismantled and sits in the infield. The water tower in the background supplies the fairgrounds, as well as the eastern section of Elkhorn.

Snow has melted off the racetrack, and the fairground is a lonely and cold place to be in Elkhorn. In a couple of months, summer will arrive and the city's anticipation will turn to the upcoming fair. The new grandstand, composed of steel and concrete, successfully accommodates thousands of fairgoers for concerts and horse races alike. For the most popular concerts, it is not uncommon for people to fill additional bleachers and the fence line around the perimeter of the track.

Ten
LIFE OF A CARNIE

For as long as anyone can remember, Farrow Amusements, a company out of Jackson, Mississippi has been delivering thrills and excitement to the fairgoers at the Walworth County Fair. Each year a newer, taller ride seems to fill the skyline of Elkhorn, along with the old standards. The images in this chapter were purchased by the author from a collection found at a Milton, Wisconsin, antique store. A carnival worker stands between the "Zipper" and the "Hurricane" in the early 1970s; note the new grandstand in the background.

The midway is located below the Ferris wheel, a much smaller model than the nearly 75-foot wheel that visits the modern fair annually.

Pictured here is a view of the landscape as the Ferris wheel takes this photographer upwards. The parking lot is on the right side, and the old Main Gate ticket booth is still standing. The ride "Swinger" can be seen below. Those with longtime connections and memories of Elkhorn may remember the old water tower; it can be seen rising from the treeline.

Above is a view of the Ferris wheel from the safety and relative comfort of the ground.

The blue and yellow tent awnings still exist after all these years. Each year the midway is filled with games of skill and chance, with the opportunity to win stuffed animals or other prizes. Here, two carnival workers await customers.

Another game offers fairgoers a chance to score a hip (at the time) fluorescent poster.

Shown here is a view of the large Ferris wheel and its past position in the center of the midway, right near the grandstand. In recent years, the ride has had its own spot alongside Highway 11 and right outside the North building. On a clear summer night during the Labor Day weekend, it is easy to spot the glow of the Ferris wheel and other rides from far outside the city.

When not partaking in the rides and the excitement of the midway, racing fans could divert their attention to the action on the track. This 1989 photograph shows a tight battle in the afternoon harness races.

Another event that draws a large crowd is the horse pulls, which use the same principles as large, fire-spurting trucks that speed down the track to see who can pull a load the farthest. In this version, powerful draft horses pull sleds with blocks. If you look closely, you can notice the board on the track tower at the finish line that lists the track's fastest records for harness racing.

Eleven
THE MODERN FAIR

This three-horse hitch hauls a smaller carriage in front of the crowd. Draft horses have become a popular attraction at the fair. During recent fairs, an entire corner of the fair has been devoted to the draft horses with a permanent building constructed and temporary tents used to house them and their caretakers, who come from all over the Midwest.

(*above*) Western hats and cowboy boots dominate the grandstand in this modern view of the current concert venue that draws fans of country music from all over Wisconsin and points beyond. The fair has traditionally hosted four days of concerts during the six-day event. The fair opens with tractor truck pulls and ends with a grand-finale, double-feature demolition derby.

(below) The crowd extends north across the grandstand, and seating becomes scarce as the start of the concert nears. Fans at the Walworth County Fair are treated to free concerts, a rarity at other county fairs. Until a few years ago, most country acts swinging into town treated fans to two shows in a single night before moving on to their next concert.

This six-horse hitch pulls a wagon down the track in front of the grandstand.

The bell tower of the Blooming Prairie School sits prominently in the park at the fairgrounds. The track is visible in the background.

A class of local school children poses in front of the steps to the Sharon Town Hall, which is located adjacent to the old schoolhouse. School children around the county get to participate in a day of class just as it would have been in a one-room schoolhouse.

Inside the classroom, students learn just as they would have years ago. Thanks in part to the Walworth County Historical Society, retired teachers take the helm at the school house and teach children, showing them how to count on an abacus, participate in spelling bees, and play games like "steal the bacon."

Another class of children poses, this time on the steps of the Blooming Prairie School. The school was constructed in 1889 and was named for the township where it was located.

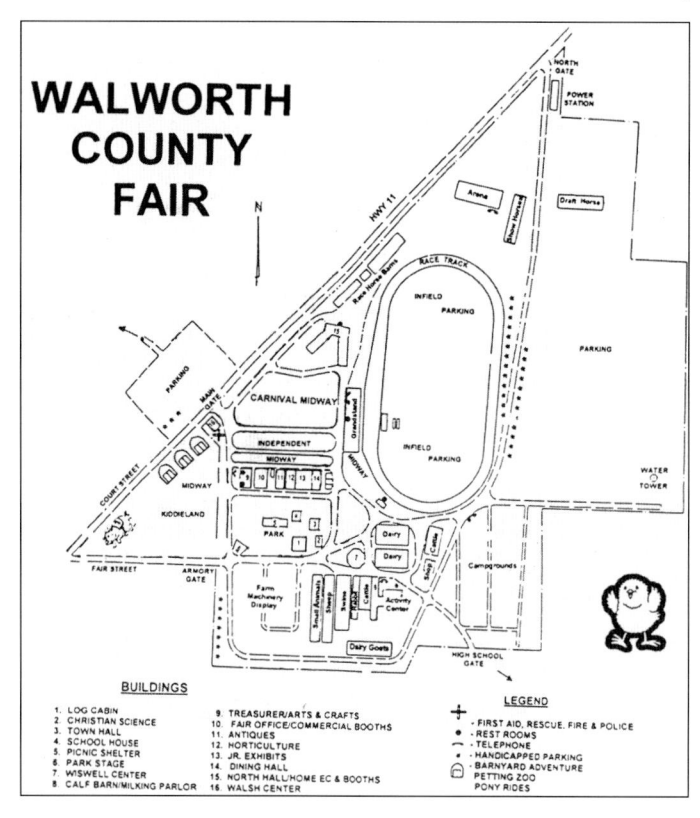

This map directs visitors so that they don't get lost while wandering the extensive grounds during the fair.

120

This 2004 image shows the lengths to which some crowds will go to get a good seat. During horse races or on-track events on the night of a particularly popular concert, fairgoers jam into the grandstand in an attempt to snag a good view or even to wait for the track to open so they can run out and stake a seat in front of the stage.

Fireworks used to deliver a bang at the fair, but it has been years since fairgoers could look up at the night sky for a light display. These days, the fair ends in a culminating, literal crash and bang when two demolition derbies tear up the track and other cars in front of the grandstand. This photograph shows the pits and the teams readying their battering ram vehicles in an attempt to win lots of prize money.

Ascending to the highest viewpoint in the fairgrounds on the Ferris wheel offers a beautiful collage of bright colors on the midway and a view of the surrounding city.

This view also shows the fairgrounds, looking southwest towards the city of Elkhorn.

Pictured here is the Ferris wheel from the perspective of the acrophobic.

From the top of the Ferris wheel looking northwest, you can see the parking lot has already reached capacity, and cars heading to the fair for the evening will be forced to scour side streets for a parking spot.

The edge of the Ferris wheel frames the image of clouds and cars far below. Pedestrians cross busy Highway 11 directly below.

Just like in the postcards from 1910, crowds still jam the streets of the midway; this time, however, they carry ears of corn, large corndogs, slices of pizza, and a variety of fried foods. This is the 2004 version of Dining Hall Row: stands line both sides of the street all the way to the grandstand in the east.

A few fairgoers brave the rain with ponchos; they have the street to themselves as they walk past the commercial booths near the fair office and the park

There's nothing better than eating your way through the fair; this man waits for his food at a taco and burrito stand in the midway.

This stunning view shows the fairgrounds at night, the rides and food stands creating a whirlwind of lights, sounds, and smells.

Kyle Adams brought both intrigue and controversy when he decided to run for the Fairest of the Fair competition. Milwaukee news helicopters hovered overhead and reporters descended on Elkhorn in 2002 when he became the first male to run in the previously all-female talent competition. Adams lost to Katie Pruessing in 1999, was runner-up in 2000, and lost in 2001.

. . . Only to grab the crown and the top honor of representing the fair all across Walworth County and Wisconsin in 2003; winners at the county fair level compete to see who can become the top representative of fairs in the state.

The Ferris wheel spins off a light show as the fair winds down for yet another night.

Elkhorn Area High School varsity baseball players call Harris Park home field. The batter's line of sight provides a lasting image of the place the fair has in the hearts and memories of Elkhorn and the county. The spur of railroad that shuttled visitors to the fair went right through this baseball field. But, until next Labor Day, the fairgrounds will remain a relatively quiet place awaiting its thunderous and joyous end of summer celebration for everyone in the county.